DEAD'S GOOD COMPANY

Other books by Judith Johnson Sherwin:

URANIUM POEMS (Yale Series of Younger Poets, 1969)
THE LIFE OF RIOT: short stories (Atheneum, 1970)
IMPOSSIBLE BUILDINGS: poems (Doubleday, 1973)
THE TOWN SCOLD: poems (The Countryman Press, 1977)
HOW THE DEAD COUNT: poems (Norton, 1978)
TRANSPARENCIES: poems (The Countryman Press, 1978)

Cassettes:

THE TOWN SCOLD (Watershed Tapes)
HOW THE DEAD COUNT (Watershed Tapes)

DEAD'S GOOD COMPANY.

(WASTE: Part Three)

Judith Johnson Sherwin

Illustrations
by
Margaret Lampe

Did all old men and women, rich and poor,
Who trod upon these rocks or passed this door,
Whether in public or in secret rage
As I do now against old age?

— William Butler Yeats, *The Tower*

The Countryman Press

TAFTSVILLE · VERMONT

Grateful acknowledgement is made to the following
periodicals, which have published or accepted for
publication some of the poems from this book:

Midwest Quarterly	"The Reckoning" "The Ghost That Walks" "Kyrie"
American Poetry Review	"Lovely Leo, Roaring Leo" "The Worth"
Sunbury	"The Deeds of Grandma Clara"
Southwest Review	"Words for Grandma Clara"
Virginia Quarterly Review	#1 of "Eight Mean Songs"
The Falcon	#3 and #7 of "Eight Mean Songs"
Connections	#4 and #5 of "Eight Mean Songs"
Poetry Now	"Count Dracula"
The Little Magazine	"A Ballad of False Comfort"
Nimrod	"The Witch of Hindustan" "Mud Poems"
St. Andrews Review	"Poem to be Thrown Away before Reading" "Poem for Max and Others"
The Helen Review	"The Wild Man of Borneo"

The title page epigraph is from the *Collected Poems* of William Butler
Yeats, and is reprinted with the permission of the Macmillan Company.
(Copyright 1924 by Macmillan Publishing Co., Inc., renewed 1952 by
Bertha Georgie Yeats.)

WASTE is a three-part sequence, written in New York and in Brussels
between 1962 and 1974. Part One of WASTE, *The Town Scold,* and Part
Two, *Transparencies,* were published by The Countryman Press in 1977
and 1978, respectively. This volume, *Dead's Good Company* (Part Three
of WASTE), completes the triptych.

CONTENTS

the Reckoning

the Sage examined the Soles of his Feet to see
who had been walking on them. no old Clothes
no cut Hair, no Excreta, Tokens of your Body,
      no Nail Pairings
shall summon out of the Wind who is not there;
no Magic shall flesh, Tradition tell, no Ritual shall enact,
oh wise Listener, you. where you are you stay, your Skin
      is not yours,
your Nails not fastened by any invisible Cord
to your emptying Hands; believe me, your Will not yours
nor mine to call; impregnable Safety stands round you,
      an unbuilt Wall.
your Footprints hold no Body in them, never did,
to cut or maim with cut Glass; even when your Feet trod
them these Grounds stayed bare.

hear them who speak without Voice or Sense, they have
something to give you
not because they were mine: they were never mine,
they were never their own, they lived and no Blood flowed
the Transparencies of their Brains; not because they shall
in their Fullness be yours, be made over to you:
      here, nothing
i say shall make you know them; Friend, not because
they're what you are and shall be, Abstracts, Ciphers,
      Shells strung
on a Cord's Clatter, Words, less than Words; for
      Words can bring

some watery Ghost to your Mind, pro Noun, but these
   shed Carapaces never shall.
they are your Winnings, your Currency, Wealth, Tokens
   of your Standing, even as i.

i send you this Reckoning from a Disaster Area
to tell you, count everything twice, the Chips fall
   where they may,
let him who has Spirit and Strength fling them away.

LOVELY LEO, ROARING LEO

play that old song for me
once more, crazy leo, on your antique
movie machine. falling down leo
the neighborhoods you booked for
have changed. they don't need your
falling down leo chains
of picture palaces, they can't use your
crazy leo crawling out in the cold
uninvited stranger's kindness toward strangers.
call it terminal depression, it's the crash
there's no picking up from, shake but you can't shake it
roaring leo, picking up the change.

it wasn't country music in the old country.
the movies, you didn't write; the language was not
good Rumanian; never mind; the taste of the public
      was different.
your poems fell down, they kicked their legs in the streets
of the language you couldn't write, of the words
      tossed away,
they were rolled, fell apart, you built them back
      word by word
once more out of country music; the chain of
      picture palaces
fell down, kicked their legs in the streets, they were
      rolled, fell apart
when you did. you didn't understand this new world.

broke, you didn't die
all passion spent. breaking the lens, leo
over the balcony onto their foreign heads.

                                        i've made good use of you,
put some of your last cacophonies into my story
of Luis Casas. this good use of you
dear leo, is no injury.

                         distributors, rivals, heirs
of this life's blacked out film, who pick through
        these leavings,
pluck out the eyes to light up your wide screens,
pull up with combs the wet chords roaring
to string your electric guitars, hear me sing out like
mad how stranger leo out in the cold
is disbursed now
to stomp out rollicking dance music for strangers
from every cash / drawer in town
                                falling down
his hoarse, accusing shouts
won't be paid out while i can keep good
count. once more, crazy man
tell us how in your own country when you were young
and roaring you were a king of poets. rag voice,
let it out loud and free.

THE DEEDS OF GRANDMA CLARA

thievery chuckles
these halls down. the memories
i sell you now were hers. i tell you
i poked in a shovel
scooped up the lamb ran golden corn
from beyond Moldavia, scooped up the blind
grandfather she led at the end of a gold tasseled
curtain pull, scooped up the gypsies
she followed into no freedom / her father's
anger, their blood over all
her stone feet, carried away
in my head streets that unloaded
the lushness, the coffins, the wolves, Count Dracula,
    Galatz,
the Danube. . .

receivers take all
the corridors away under wraps, the rattle. . .
the necklace of teeth i rattle
against my gums was hers
the bracelets of bones that play
under the skin of my wrists, loosely / when
she had the use of them, knotted,
worked dolls, worked children, worked blind
    grandfathers, gypsies
all over my pillow, knotted the streets of Galatz
into my hair, knotted the blood of the gypsies
into my stone, knotted the scalps of her children,

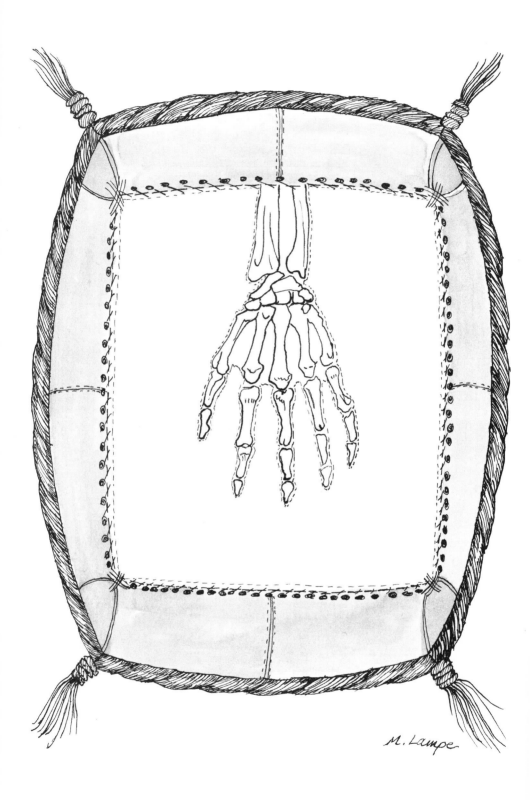

M. Lampe

my mother and aunts / into her dried drumhead
knuckles that now i wear /
                    and they dangle there
they dangle there.

my trophies. my powers of attorney.
my signatures. my deeds. my authority.
she who witnessed
her grandfather's blind conveyances out of his head
has no power to see herself
go that way. she is
stripped. last night i pressed both thumbs
down on her wrinkled moon eyelids
            (while the Count in blood hunger opened up
            his red maw, drooled by her pillow)
popped out the eyes, took them away
in a clear, plastic bag.
                    no one stopped me.

WORDS FOR GRANDMA CLARA

Grandma Clara won't lie still.
Grandma Clara feels unwell.
you've got her mind. if you know
what's good for you you'll let it go.
you'll bring back the words too.
with corners of her mouth stitched shut
Grandma Clara is no fool.
though she has no words to tell
her anger out, her eyes can roll
blindly, blindly on a string.
if you bring back all you stole,
       if you come to pity her
Grandma Clara gently, gently
       hopes you will
though now her mouth keeps opening, closing
before next winter rot in hell.

EIGHT MEAN SONGS

M. Lampe

ONE: SHE'S WAITING THE NIGHT OUT

for my grandmother

she's waiting the night out, old and shapeless, it
    won't happen
shrill, voice scratching at you
            that any new flower will open
in one of the pots by the window, sing hallelu
into her sickbed mind. the sun that sprouts
at the top of one of the weedstalks out there, the Pan Am
building, or one of the others,
won't bring good news to her
get the world out of its closet, shake the bones out, shout
sweet sister you're not through
            (the old complaint
             i share with her:
             your daughters don't love you
             have other things to do
since you were the starling chattered in their ears
of gold all the way to every coast
your white decked mind could touch on. (she grunts: *they*
             back when, yes, had
             clean hands to shake out for me
             two good friends to lay about me
when they plucked the strings that made me flap
i whispered of silver winds and the jeweled
eyes of fishes rolled in the deep
            it's the old voice
            of angry bitches
            and with it i know how
            to chew out the roots in windy ditches
            as if they did it: *my old man*
            is changed, my two girls changed their skins
            i don't know what
                    i have

Two: The Little One's Song

for my daughters

what, nobody killed this year? quick, tonto, before
someone puts us down as a major fuckup, kill
leroy jones, gun down
george wallace, whoopee, dispose
of the *Grandeur* of france with his mouth full
                        (fat lady down on my floorboards croaks
                         braiding a brandnew mop of hair:
                         my little one sings all day
                         lucy in the sky with die-ins
of bomb blast bombast, dot
dayan one for me in his good eye *she's got no use for you*
                         baby she's not yet two
                         one thing sure, one of them, your child or
                              mine won't live past three
then slip your slicer in nasser *well the child*
                         don't need me
                         baby she just turned three
don't let the new sun   *the day this black child turns four*
                         she won't want this world no more
go down on you
without you get
a big one for grandpa death

12

Three: The Starling's Song

for the buyers

and sings, hoarse, gross, love, last
night i was the starling chattered in your ear, and you
packed me up while the winds played fair
in the bloody currents of your desires
you became a rifle to bang out fear through
each whistlestop in the gobi desert
my humped ship skidded down every oil
hole you played me, and yet we left
no slimy trail but a white wake
and a foaming good cheer shout`of joy
when we slid over the little fishes
jellied in innocence.
                  there's
a man standing where it all happened more than a year ago
he doesn't want what i want, and he knows what i know
he laughs when i simper, girlish, *the world's my beau*

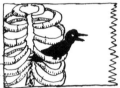

a new fashion in sweat has just come out
this year, last year, when i wasn't looking. that crumpled
old ball of stuff, glamour gone, let me tell you i just
scooped it up in a big heat, closed a fist
on the whole torn gas of it, into the dark with it, bang.
the old horrors i wore
till they hung on me like skin
don't fit right no more. i've gone and bought
the new look, the wet look, the not quite dead look,
    swings
differently when i shake with it, somebody maybe
in Paris said last year's blood
can't be seen in me it moves so bad, and what
i want needs a new shape under it. i've got to run
somewhere, buy a new self to wear this life
before they're all sold out.

Four: There's A Man Standing

for jimmy

there's a man standing where it all
                              and the words
the great-bellied sailing words cut up
as he slides by
and where the hairs on my neck feather out
he tells himself
just slant of the corner of each eye
lightly along reckoning of my skin
where last night sounding the night
in me, big-handed singular terror sang:
*we're going to stay here always, listen, we've set
down bones in this, can't pull out*

hoarse, gross, love, last
night i was the fairhaired candidate
the oilrag to polish your big stick
i had positions to give away
and a great gold-pointed spiked crown
to see me through to the light of day
i was the babydoll brandished a knife
at your bouncing prow with a fresh-minted two-headed
medal for every lady's man
who clapped his hands at the show of force
then you became a razorblade / cut me down quick

i thought the death in me all dried
up, bawled, like pip pop hemingway, one
finger tight on the trigger, the gun hole set
to my mouth, to my shrink: *hey tonto,
it just won't come anymore, afternoon or no time,
gotta cry, bye-bye.*

back from my dream of the Great Bad Place
(for it i had left you, true,
with a bed of herring for your kin
merry as a mackerel under sea)
all that i was / back
lips i thrust out on their stalks to kiss

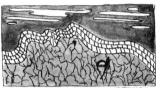

where it all happened more than a year ago
the bald, plucked Creature, lay / crumpled beside
he doesn't want what i want, and he knows what i know
and shuddering, pulls back his headless into its pearl
shell, peace, with a wicked, denying twitch.
it is the same world still.

he is my love in the out of doors
and under the clinging kneeholes of desks
squats, knees hitched up and one nail raised,
scratches, *awrk*

        well you
hip-swishing miniworld don't cry
we'll get you a new love by and by

FIVE: YOU, LOVE, THE SAD REVOLUTIONARY

for myself

voice scratching the dirt deep
down she plants her man:
you with your ordered life
intricate, neat
controlled as a bach suite
tomorrow nightmare will come true
help, you'll chew through thicks of black
in your mouth, and nobody saves you

i count the faces of those i loved
whose minds i plundered when nothing else
could answer me but the wide
slap of nothing across my will
those i used and couldn't sleep
till their nightbreeze indies eyes were mine,
lit up the harbor that never was / *quick*

> before

you became a razorblade / cut me down quick

you, love, the sad revolutionary
keep your place in the sun,
not meaning to, go round
with the same fixed crowd
of herring, the same damned round
with your ordered life
thought the death in me all dried

NOT   TOO   LOUD

you'll wake the Man
grunts: *i've been around*
made this scene, don't want
one   /   more   /   sound
breaking my thisyear sleep

> nobody here to tell me
> what i already knew
> nobody here to tell you
> what i'm not going to
> an open, easy, free hate
> still a long way

16

SIX: THE USER'S SONG

for the sisters

those stranger voices i used till they grew mine
                              you say you don't
look into it, you who think
what you are must be unique   *like the way they half rhyme.*
once you were the wolf whooped *woof woof*
at every wind's shimmy that shook my strings
what i was i couldn't make
till every good
mind i touched had sprung a leak

this came to me without prayer
beyond hope, from every spent *put them away and say*
                              well nobody's buying you today
soul and i was merry
quick as a mackerel under sea
jolly as a pheasant under glass
i danced at your prow all set
to make an end / praise God *go way till somebody calls you*

                    and you left me there and you left me there
that i could be land's end

SEVEN: YOU HIP-SWISHING MINIWORLD DON'T CRY

for the magicians

well you hip-swishing miniworld don't cry
we'll get you a new man by and by

he is my love who under the snapping stars
in the fair trade of broad noon shoots out
his reptile neck and sneers
and i have written to him in the Great Bear
out of the side-stepping Crab's claws
stung by the Scorpion's tail
and riding the white foam wings of the Flying Horse
a letter he will not understand
though he scan it with all his light years

EIGHT: SKIN-CHANGER'S SONG

for all of us

what animal we've been, how many nights
and not done yet with skin
we're going to stay here always, my dear, the pit
is hallowed where we drop
ape-jaw and molar in, witch-croak, what we were
(and under the tree we are) sunken,
diamondback snake scales shed
rockslides ago and still
wearing us, the green venom jet
is hallowed we were that day
and i remember well
if i will not have you i must have him

COUNT DRACULA

it isn't hunger, exactly, for blood or life.
i would stop if i could and lie / underground.
senseless activity lifts me, pulls me around,
floats me in through your window, spills me alive
out of the mist to what called me. i'm not my own.
believe me, lady, i come to your body's smell
which thunders the summons. if i hadn't come in
you'd have had to invent me. teach your blood to
        run quietly
and i can lie down again no more than a dream
of an old   /   action

                 played out.

for Betty, dead of cancer

A BALLAD OF FALSE COMFORT

they neither kneel to pray for me
nor take their comfort stretched at length
but they that love me rest their bones
shank by shank on a stone bench

uneasiness and lust of hours
sing out the watch you keep
eight o'clock and all's well
nine o'clock and time you sleep

nine days: desire is tireless
nine weeks: weariness to wait
i shall outlast your hunger; look,
nine months and not done yet

sure we have dreamed the hour away
i slept and so was brought to bed
rise up, rise up good mourners all
comfort me now i am dead

                    teeth to the dog
                    horns to the deer
                    and to the dead
                    dead wood to wear

                    box for the bones
                    cold space for breath
                    grey stones
                    the bridal wreath

earth to press heavy
on your breast
weight of love
to make you rest

why do you wake
you should sleep
we have too much
of you to keep

"it's narrow, narrow keep your bed
dear brother, for my sake,
for the chill hours sheeted me
years so you need not lack

it's naked may you wear your skin
for me, my sister's child,
i have made pain my intimate
to clothe you from the cold."

"if we have eaten and are full
and lie down warm in bed
are you more sick when we are well
because we live are you more dead?

cast down, cast down your body's load
throw off all lust to give
learn to lie easy under stone
we took all from you and we live."

M. Lampe

cut from the skull
a cup of skill
the bridegroom then
may take his fill

from fingers' ends
and bones in wrist
sharp necklace
for the bride we'll twist

but the soft parts
heart brain and loin
no human thing
shall use again

dearest, don't keep
that body sweet
we live and feast
on living meat

they neither bless the bread they break
nor praise the wine they swill
yet i that lie here swollen cry
how still my belly is not full

if i that lust for what i lost
could have the world to eat
would i lie cold as i have lived
torn for another's meat

oh brother, sister, make my bed
make it deep and wide
lay a stone garland at my head
that i may die a bride

that i may die a bride my dear
who never was a wife
and all the creatures under earth
praise God that i had life.

THE WILD MAN OF BORNEO

spitted by spines of itch upon
one leg, i scratched until i'd made
a scab, then scratched the scab away.
the swamps of Borneo chuckled through
my orange hair and chattering walk.
green fur of the jungle trees fell out
in clumps / each hairy bush and vine
waved its sinuous arms for joy
when i clawed my ulcer till it bled
then howled at that lush mortality.

LEO, CLARA, MAX

old men, old woman. the demented,
the dying, the dead are in me. i can't
get clear of them or exhaust them. see

the arrogance of death, that turning away
that washing of hands. he's passing us all up, he
is cold, he's vicious, he's stubborn,
stupid, opinionated.
in Daniele Crespi's cruel portrait

the dead monk sticks out his knobby
jaw, a fighter: his hardware
spread out, the nostrils flare
        the lips sneer, contempt
lurches in his bones' set
        how he shifts his weight
how he slants his forehead back
into the unshown, tilts
his domed skull, turns his thought
away from us, hides it
tosses his mind out

oh / fear-crazed world / oh
fear-crazed world

who would be as he
no meaning, all
gesture: no cushion, no roundness
to take you, to answer you, all hard ground
surface, counter, triumph
of not / needing

the spine, the steering
column, the head, the wheel, the will
on its stalk turning
me, turning me
away. there's
what may be a sun, an explosion
that won't take me far, there's
what may be an old wrecked car
that can't / lay this body down

oh / fear-crazed world / oh
fear-crazed world

leo clara max
my mumbled outbursts, my thought-
out wits, who judged me for my
disorders, passed up distortion
and frenzy, lived sweet reason
i won't
reassemble you, polish you, make you
live / for anyone.

you have been
sane but i promise, you shall be
mad always / you have had
properties of mass and weight but you shall
splash flat and be stain
only. now you must climb
the hairy stairs of the iron tower whose moss
treads clasp your feet in their green
formless   /   borrowing
of shape, but i say you shall find
by God's good means the grace
to fall

    oh / fear-crazed world / oh
         fear-crazed world

THE WITCH OF HINDUSTAN

i thought i couldn't find the grace
to be a ghost without a mind
so made a magical, noisy place
where i could chant myself blind.
chains of atoms hung the cave
winds in rhythm chimed a spell
that made each calcium toothlet spill
its lime for me. my images gave
the sign and i worshipped them as God.

caught in my twitching, spinal void
more resonant than alchemy
i praise this world's electric night.

i have loved rhetoric more than my own mind
and dance here stupidly, stupidly, like a word.

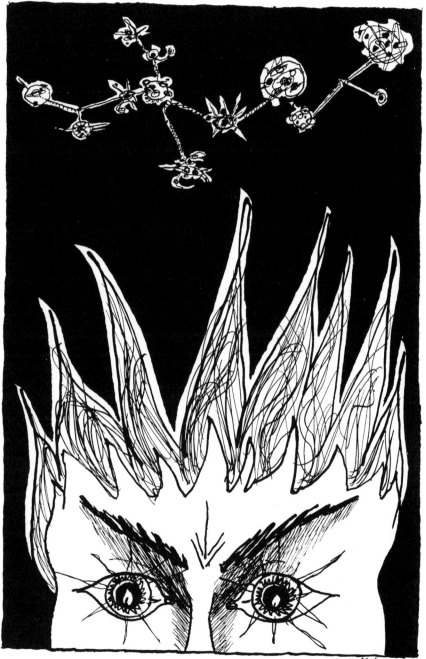

MARJORIE

1

everyone i love is so much more human
warmer than i am. what i do
with tension and heaving effort, like an ape pushing
     a loaded
shopping-cart through the mud, not knowing what's
     in it,
you do as easily   /   as floating.

          marjorie, i don't know
          if the poems you sent me were good
          or dreadful. you may be far ahead or outside
          of all of us. as thought, they seemed crazy to me,
          as gesture inept, as offering self-centered:
          your poem, "White on White on White,"
               so abstract
          the words paled to ash before i could read
          sense into them.
                         muzzy with certainty of your call
          you tossed out as blank irrelevancies
                                   all mere chime
          of discipline / of sound, of sense, of proportion.

this before i was born
and you still young.

2

i would ask you to hold still, ask you to come down awhile
ask you to speak simply
i would ask you what sealed-off passages in your skull
                              as in others i love
what garden, what moon green
lunacy pushed up through

your brainpan to break you open before i was born
ask you to speak simply as a child

    i've seen you maybe three times
in my life, and the first two you scared me.
        stone deaf,
eyes unfocused, head turning continually
                    and the inarticulate
                            speech
of one who for years had felt no voice enter: i
    thought
you a witch or the ghost of mist.
                    later i felt contempt. nine
                       years old,
smug in my party-dress and my mother's worship,
i played piano, giggled, made faces, struck
    wrong notes
on purpose. your words slurred past me
                      toneless
                      terrible
as any holding thing that has no body
                    is terrible
no handhold   is terrible, melts
speaks with no mouth, with mind only speaks,
    with will speaks,
the current will, with a leaping spark speaks
from the mind to the mind and into the central blank
pulsing nervous listening readiness stings
    singes, burns out everything,
                  but speaks:

    don't   /   do   /   that
    when you play i can feel   /
                   notes in the air.

                                     clearly
and simply as a child
             always
                  i've told you
in letters what i'd want no one alive to hear.

3

you wrote me once that the earth
of deafness you'd been since childhood was God's proof
of His gifts in you, that the pale clay clods
He'd tumbled by spadefuls over your sight must
      be touchstones:
                        the spinning world
       of dizziness, spots in the eyes, white, buzzing,
confusion, to change shape, spots in the memory, white,
buzzing, dilating, to fill time, eyes to change time,
               targets, bullseyes, centers
          to white out time, not black it
signs hot to spell wherein lay
your worth /
        muttered in your housing of silence, you did
not speak to be heard or loved or understood.

    why, lady, you pushed from your way as foppery
    all thought to answer your time, to answer to
       any time;
    doggedly writing poems you showed no one
    you refused, as a legacy of thrift, that flat demand
    any ritual makes that you touch on something solid.
    dizzied with an abstract, orbiting intellect,
    you wouldn't be held to earth,
                   you were
                     earth

if not earth then some greater body, a sun
    broken loose
beyond glass to see, beyond system to hold,
    beyond chart to measure the path.
each year brought you closer to mastering your
    trajectory:
to lay waste every talent your great
achievement. dear priestess of emptiness
what had you to do with making anything clear
in your years of stone, in your bleached metal tides
and ruined worlds, in your tongue-tied eloquence.

                        reverberations
of thought, concentric, shot out of line,
exploded, fell flaming when you burst out
of your four wits' brilliance to batter down
intelligence. garbled, drowned in ores of vowels,
constricted in consonants that couldn't work clear,
                images wrought to set
that hot spirit in you melted, exercise
of choice blew out. God's deafening silence broke
with your gabbling
    oh blackening radiance of effort
to utter such stars, such sunburst flowers, such
    blue-white
  hard-bright fountains of steel, such fireworks
of no utterance through a mouth
                stopped with its own tongue.

wit's candles, you blazed, weren't worth a pin
without your head to gutter in.

4

you sent everything
and i haven't answered, more than three years now,
                    my voice choked off like yours,
but when i write letters to any / friend to bring love
                    to pray pardon
to contemplate great pain, or confess my dumb failures
at answering love with love
                    i speak to you

who would send this back unread
as you have done before
simply as a child

        if i thought i couldn't write
        wit's blankness before i was burnt out
        or holy madness until my sense
        had gone to keep yours company
        i didn't know the sacred light
        death keeps in me
                    to white out as suns white out
        as the ghost of ash whites out
        black suns of the mind, pulse beyond instrument
        we know by the light it bends
        or breaks in the silent height
        and life and eye of the star-
        storm light, white on white on white

i come down to some feel of the poem
as act, as waste, as throwing away, the final / plenty
                                    as dying
before we die

        and the poems
        you sent have been good to me.

THE GHOST THAT WALKS

they're old, that man who made me up, and those who
    first listened.
they were never good for much. the banality
of a self-defeating life was all they could touch,
but i follow them, hissing, from every blasted mind.
give beauty back, Hopkins said, and i say he was right
i have no need to be seen, i walk in the night
listen, i have no voice, nothing to say,
they're mad, and they mutter me, mutter me like a play.

their beautiful, cracked voices make me sing
shake over the night of the jungle / as wind shakes
    in a string

because these ghosts have cast away their sense
as if it weighed no more than straw
i've laughed at originality
and thrown off every brilliance. wit
and pride of craftsmanship i knew
when i walked in my flesh like you
must be as ditches in the rain
and every muddied pavingstone
sound to my bodiless tread before
stripped to one clear, unspeakable wail
i pierce into those i praise like an awl
and stand to put on my skills again.

their beautiful, cracked voices make me sing
shake over the night of the jungle / as wind shakes
    in a string

36

MUD POEMS

"Tu m'as donné ta boue et j'en ai fait de l'or."
— Baudelaire

1

i dreamed and in my dream
lay healing   mud
bubbled up out of everyone like jewels: red mud
from Red Mountain in Aspen, clay mud
blistered my children's eyes, green mud
moss on those waiting to die, gold mud
crusted the mummy's bones in the glass case

> you'd taken my head off
> to show to the neighbors. it was
> the third time that week i had to get
> a new head. it's a fine head.
> bright. it shines
> in the sun. it comes clean
> in the rain. it doesn't wash
> away. i dream of when
> i'll carry your head round
> to my friends. who'll say
> that's a fine head too.
> made for you.

2

before i came to this city
of eaters i saw max
    in his nursinghome green room, nursinghome dirty
    jewel in a shriveled box, the voice
    that made me laugh once
    a senile gibber. couldn't tell
    whose hand yanked him up by the scalp, peeled
    the skin back from the brain, laid bare
    the soft parts, let the air blow
    the foam thoughts
      out of him
        stripped the skull

before i saw max i saw
grandma clara rock her cluttered
    cube, nursinghome blowsy.
    hair crazy with all neglect, wits tangled,
    will uncombed, she whined her hate
    of children grandchildren mothers
    fathers sisters brothers
    who count their change, who keep
    moving, who leave her where
    she is

3

we sing
sober songs here, we praise hardened arteries
and thank senility / for they have spared
    us cancer.
reverently
we complain of some uncounted
loss, impartially
we hate each other, we shoot
antiseptic greetings at visitors
as if the plague lives in them
by inheritance, by imitation
by choice, as it lives in me.

what is there, what can we say, what can we make
of our lives, you whom i love, and how,
that won't turn foul
when we let air in on it, won't smell
when we hold it awhile, won't fall
apart when we touch it, won't lose its shape
when we look   /   closely, won't fit too well
to move in, hang too loose
to hold our flesh to us, be too loud
for everyday wear, get shrill
when the bad fit of long living
takes it   /   publish
the tally of all our losses
in this mud mountain / how shall we cut it
when it wails like that

i am real
gentle i don't say
there is no way

4

if we grow into
a questionable maturity, like cheese
or coal, without having grown
grace, i don't say
there is no way
if we articulate
the skeleton, then hang over it what was not
given us, i don't say
there is no way
if we sweat to construct
not grace but a polished, grinning
imitation of grace
that will outlast the shiver
and taking flesh of grace, i don't say
there is no way

5

i move
into my falling apart
with hatred in the bones
of idiocy, i shake
an unfriendly grin of welcome at you. see
            in the eyeholes,
            the temples, the arched portals
            of nostrils, the ruined porch
            of the mouth, the cracked columns
            of speech, the shining fissures
            where thought danced in a metal robe,
                shot out sunspears
            at you, you shall need no alchemy
            no sweetening, no spice, no hammered out
            covering
                    i bring you

mud on both hands
and the fingers broken off, i bring you
mud of the bowels and groin, mud
eyes that crawl down my cheeks to blacken
my mouth, mud lips
that leave wet marks on you. the mud
is flesh. the mud is lust.
the mud is tenderness
and anger. dear heart i give
my mud to you, don't say you'll change it
to gold.

POEM TO BE THROWN AWAY

BEFORE READING

because
it's an act, a deed of gift, not a set of anything,
because images, words, are idols to this imbecile truth,
i've said: *let my poems be rambling, discursive, loose,
they shall be full.* don't look, i'm giving you everything,
    all
abundance is yours to take in this space
and tear up and not see because
it's nothing. the act alone
what i praise.

      if our lives could be like that.

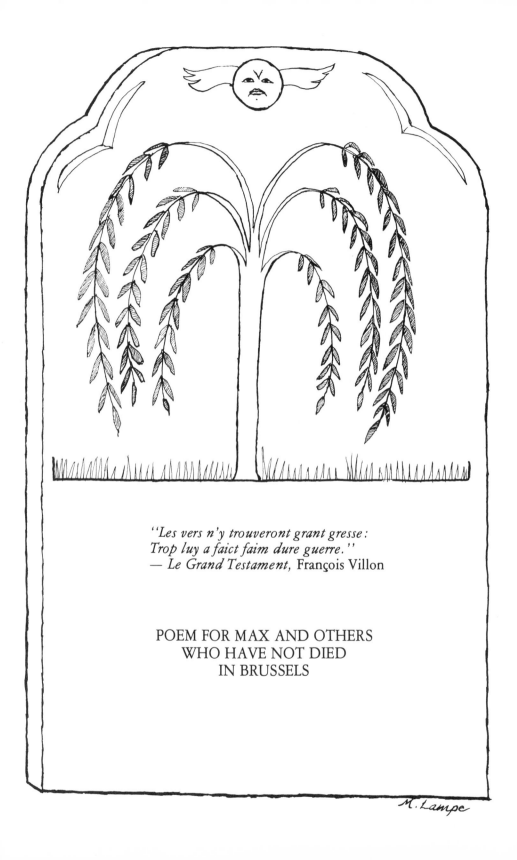

"*Les vers n'y trouveront grant gresse:*
Trop luy a faict faim dure guerre."
— *Le Grand Testament,* François Villon

POEM FOR MAX AND OTHERS
WHO HAVE NOT DIED
IN BRUSSELS

M. Lampe

come on down with me, come down
from that clean room at the top of your head
talk of cheese / talk of wine
let me teach you Brussels, teach you to smell
Brussels where i lie far / from you, common
    market square
on a buying selling eating drinking greedy-come-
    lately jag
frites jabber rapid fire
from stalls on the corners / sell you the grease of days
    cheeses hung
from the rafters rot into ripeness
eaten with their own life
    hams hung
in a row knock out the hour
shank rapping at shank / or
    belly to ass, jar
      their dull thump call to prayer
          this
friend, is how Brussels is done

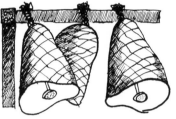

      ah yes
in Brussels they made me a good grease
a rich spread to grace any feast
last night *ils me trouvèrent grant gresse*
geule et fesse they are
machines to eat and excrete, "conceived
(said Baudelaire, when he lived here) in drunkenness,
    born

44

in excrement.'' nor sensual tongue
nor knowledge of pleasure here, nor
joy of gluttony, but they are bound
fast to a catalog
of joyless discriminations, one year and the next,
vintage, slope, cellar, a sullen
yammer for classification swallows them whole
while the cheeses cry: *God*

> *have mercy on us your poor*
> *saints here we have hung*
> *rung in a row our bells under*
> > *Brussels rain*
> > > *this many a year*
> *slung in our crossed ropes*
> *drummed our bald yellow*
> *pates one on another the wind*
> *has scraped our eyelids clean*
> *of scum and the rain has scrubbed*
> > *us down*
> *ham shackled to ham the wild*
> *boar out of Ardennes Forest roars*
> > *his pain*
> *into our sides we have known*
> > *no good*
> *time nor forbearance of anyone*

> *God hear us,* the wines cry
> through the babble of blood pressed
> from the Congo: *did each kind slope*
> *lie out to stretch under your heat,*
> > *each hill*

grow tangled to comb, to braid
green tresses
over the frames of your thought,
did your careful sun pour
gold liquor and lather of perfume
down
on their acreages / annointing
them, lord
God, all that vigorous
rich heat / shrunk to a food train
to bring a good grease to Brussels
town?

this chattering
fat in which i live, by which i die

POEM WRITTEN ON A TRAIN,

MOVING,

MAD,

to talk of the dead like this,
jeer at any celebration had power or will
to keep them late with us, whether
an ode to François Villon, to Jane
Austen, maiden, long gone
in commerce with earth, or that poem to James Dean
died yesterday. they are all dead, equally

absent, irrelevant, blot, unless / we raise them. see
    how we
sunken in the rank holes of the cheeses / of Brussels,
    swung round in their wheels
are / resurrection. i now am
fame, the kiss of time

over all these dead, fanning the hairs back
of their necks, marking their polished
foreheads with steam of my breath. whom
i stain with my mind, Max,
that man lives
        eats old cheese
                drinks the young may wine
                    can shit
again, will touch
quartz and persimmons, but
whom i put out of mind must die
go thou, do likewise in Brussels under the sky
who ripens all evenly
in the end, you choose your dead / i choose mine

POEM, THEREFORE, FOR

FRANK O'HARA, KENNETH KOCH

AND WHOMSOEVER NEEDS IT

you also to step
off that gallows where Villon hung, go
down where Jane Austen, James Dean are one /
    chew the fat
of being dead, you also to go
rehearsing glorious laughter

going back over it, over it, each time
the way Brussels is done, that's how we make dead
dead rhyme, part of the blood, makes it clot, but still
is not, God knows, the deciding factor.
my head held high on a pike can write
even as Cromwell's, and having writ
moves on, ok, but i do, i can, can something more,
    can go back
now, i cancel it, i redo the whole damn / business,
    i cancel your death

even now before you have it home free
with you. while you're thinking of something /
          else, busy, not listening, maybe absent-
               mindedly making love
in a word, you can hear, if you will
at your back / me with a cold blast
out of Brussels hurrying near
to take your death away
share it out:
               now death will not keep you straight
                    not in any line
not any day

POEM FOR MAX, WAITING

     old wreckage, story-teller
     small as a baby's skin
     dried, pasted onto a frame to wilt
     on the Mad Anatomist's desk, you
     crooked, seams of your naked
     cover sewn carelessly, all the stuff
     of you puckered when you crawled
     into it, you who refused
     all of it, pushed love round on your plate,
          finicky,
     left / all of us
     over

(only the children
you gulped down in that lunatic
insatiable thriller you ran
friday nights
      through three generations
       of heads
            the country
Ibsen, Napoleon,
your heroes, walked hand in hand
      and upside-down
with John Givitzski Bizarre
while His Cousin The Great Mahaar
in impartial disgust at all ambulation
made everyone cool it)

       puffed
eighty years on the same cigar
its embers drilling your vest

you, skimpier
than my seven
year old daughter, stringy as a starved
weed on a garbage mind in Old China,
wispy, shredded, been through the grater
eighty times with all the nothing you've had
tell me
when did any who loved you give you food
for joy

ROLLCALL

is frank o'hara Dead
i don't know frank o'hara
is kenneth koch Dead
i don't know kenneth koch
is allen ginsberg Dead
i don't know allen ginsberg
is robert bly Dead
hey, robert, i still have your pained / letter
   "these poems are awful" some were, some
      weren't, well
is james dean Dead
james, are you Dead, please talk to me
is jane austen Dead
jane, tell me now
is françois villon Dead
whom paris found *grant gresse*
as brussels me, say
is judy sherwin Dead
is carol bergé Dead
no carol, not you, not you, girl, not you dead,
   no no not
      carol, sharp voice, short angry hair,
        sure
      intolerant eyes loving me / with a
        love clean as
      hatred, dark, fierce stance, far
      now, can't hear me, busy bugging
        your friends,
      cheering your enemies, have to get
        everyone right
      this minute, can't wait, not carol /
        Dead
      loveliness

who's Dead then, who's Dead that i know
i don't know Dead, he's
something else, he's nobody, can't phone Dead
say, friend, Dead, help me
find some good word for max, now every good
grease is a bad grease where i've come to
this rollcall

LITANY

POEM IN MEMORY / OF DEAD

                    but
i have been one acquainted, sometimes, with that
old fart, i know Dead intimately
i've sucked him off, he's sucked me
such pleasure we've shared with the lights blown out
brought betty low as her cancer
who lies in the earth now
i know his habits, know how
to tickle him, tell exactly
how he'll come, how he'll scream, what convulsion,
grab my thigh with his teeth, Dead
Dead, Dead, i holler, i know you, buddy, let's
lie down   /   together

why yes, he's Dead, that guy over there
not you, he's the one, he's
Dead, smell that gravesweat, solemn
with fumes of seven swamps / of meaning, the breath
bloat, heavy with what's been
written off him, look at the long green
teeth eating the cheesy
cheeks / he's
gone all the way
Dead is all there

Poem Written under the Influence
of Everybody

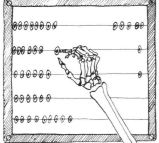

when you add
me to your slate, try to see
the grin, knobby hand, lollypop stick
fingers that finger you.
i count you, dearly beloved
whom i know, whom i don't know
whom i gather
merely

candy-cane striped, mottled, chocolate, gooey, come
    off on my fingers,
whom i hold too long, melt down, oh you goodies,
    how sweet
to be Dead, enjoy our good taste together. let's go
Dead now
    lie down, Dead, lie down
in Dead's good company, cavernous
easy to love head, play games in there, roar
into the mountains of never
Dead, in a crazy exuberance

your voices, Dead
grow in me lazy
lying down pleasures, your fingers, Dead, smashed
tendons for all time, from your slick slug
cock, i soak up the rumble
of wheels sliding through me, the train shrill
makes me   /   *squeal*

POEM FOR MAX, WAITING
for DEAD TO GIVE HIM A MIND
OR TWO

the Witch of Hindustan
has got you in her mean
black rock cunt, when you stir
squeezes you; the Wild
Man of Borneo
huge, stooped, fringed like a fat armchair
all over his seams, red swinging hair
and arms of a Flying Carpet
the deep puffy cushions of his neck swollen over
his shoulders, he's gone
in his great, squat yellow square
back teeth, crunched your mind like a nut
hoo ha, uncle max
the Ghost That Walks is here
just back of your wishbone shoulder, leans
into you, whispers your hair
through his oozing fingers, wheezes
his papery laugh while you chant
your prayer:

baby-baby
i can't see, i can't hear, baby-baby
i can't see, i can't hear, baby-baby
i can't see, i can't hear
baby-baby   /   baby-baby

the night your hands let drop the cigar
your legs burned clear through the yellow bone to the
    marrow / your head
        cleaned out, Dead, come now
        tenderly, eagerly, greedily
        with a great fiery roar
        of orgasm for my uncle
        max who made no woman
        or child in his tenderness
        take him

POEM GOING TO FIRENZE ON A TRAIN

Firenze   Frenzy   Firenzy   Frenze   Firenze   Frenzy

unwillingly
stubbornly
it forces me
what do i see
and not know
poetry

let me blast you off the face
of the earth, my contemporaries
who will not take
a piss without stopping that first
easy, direct fizz to determine
whether it's academic

now while you count
vintage, year, slope, and how the sun runs this season
its race of poem, while you gobble
theory, manifesto, everything but / the poem, like
    an explosion
of french intellectuals, while you spend your fire
to reckon for Dead / who won't measure up

let's finish ourselves, end all of us, end
mouthing ourselves, take off now,
skin, bone, mind, will, all
categories that keep us
partial, insular, take
this ode back to its title, say we made it
rest   /   together

FOR MAX WHO IS NOT DEAD

       in Dead's indiscriminate
       rocket hysteria
       of enjoyment, who is
       the poem alive in all
       its titles, its right
to move, is / those titles. what can we do now
with this immensity, oh icon, oh monster, oh hairy /
    animal
        scratching, whining, oh / calculations, oh
           plenty, oh splendor
        of ending with no / dignity, oh messy right
         of passage through / form
         into generosity

POEM
WITH SOME SEVERAL TITLES
TO DEATH

THE WORTH

oh my loved my hated my nearly alive
and dead
do i expose you now
by name to a crowd
for nothing / poor demented
take from you even the last goods
life left, your good name

        i've heard you talk on
        past sense and not listened
        my mind full of my / mind
        my mind   my mind
        my mind that incantation

i don't know you
i swear i never knew
you or who you were

will you be angry at me
will you think i could have sent out
almost the same bad
tally and named no names
every word i write may be the lie
of a pinched spirit
to clear my books   /   no way

if you see how i use you

        not that any stranger
        may   remember
        these figures that are not yours

before you die
will this make all good
for you: in every lie
set down here
        like truth
i say and say and say
my only worth
your dear names
        like a prayer

KYRIE

the oldest stones / hear them talk to me tonight,
paid-out stars with no glow who have slowed themselves
    into rock,
foamed out of silence fires, hard minds and hearts
gold unmalleable, and now fall, shriveled, back
    into silence,
bent wrinkled coins forspent and dense as time:
hear how frozen those bodies' dark weight breaks light
    open, how far
those minds count and recount their heaviness out of
    the scarred-
home craters, forgiven, past giving, where light
    swallows light:

they tell what true metal that night is they have held
until its clear fires cooled in them past clay /
tell all out: how good our hottest stars shall make
the world's waste, keep back nothing / tell and tell
how in that great generosity of death
we shall give out and burn our minds away.